A DORLING KINDERSLEY BOOK
Conceived, edited, and designed by DK Direct Limited

Note to parents

What's Inside? Spacecraft is designed to help young children understand the wonders of space travel. It shows them how a rocket gets into space, what it is like to travel in a lunar module, and how astronauts manage to spend months on a space station. It is a book for you and your child to read and talk about together, and to enjoy.

Editor Hilary Hockman
Designers Helen Spencer and Juliette Norsworthy
Typographic Designer Nigel Coath
U.S. Editor Laaren Brown

Illustrator Richard Ward
Photographers Geoff Dann and James Stevenson
Written by Alexandra Parsons
Consultant Nicholas Booth
Design Director Ed Day
Editorial Director Jonathan Reed

First American Edition, 1992

10 9 8 7 6 5 4 3 2 1

Published in the United States by
Dorling Kindersley, Inc., 232 Madison Avenue
New York, New York 10016

Library of Congress Cataloging-in-Publication Data
Spacecraft. – 1st American ed.
    p. cm. – (What's inside?)
    Summary: Examines the inner workings of various spacecraft,
including the rocket, command module, and space shuttle.
    ISBN 1-56458-136-5
    1. Space vehicles – Juvenile literature. [1. Space Vehicles.]
I. Series.
TL793.S658 1992
629.4 — dc20   92–52832 CIP AC

Printed in Italy

WHAT'S INSIDE?
SPACECRAFT

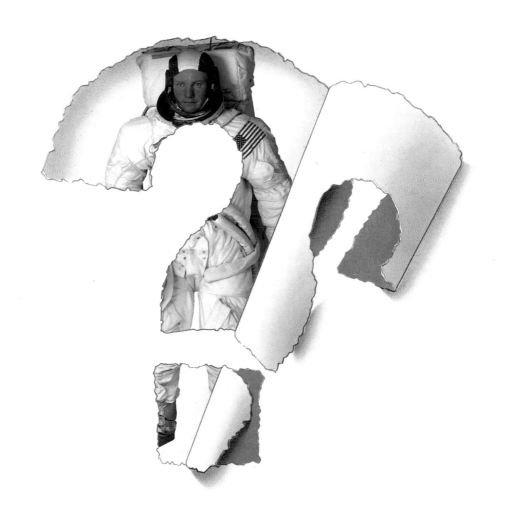

DK

DORLING KINDERSLEY, INC.
NEW YORK

ROCKET

This American *Saturn 5* rocket took the first astronauts to the Moon. To get into space it had to shoot up in the air at high speed and break free of Earth's gravity – the force that pulls things back to Earth. Then it could push on through the airless space beyond.

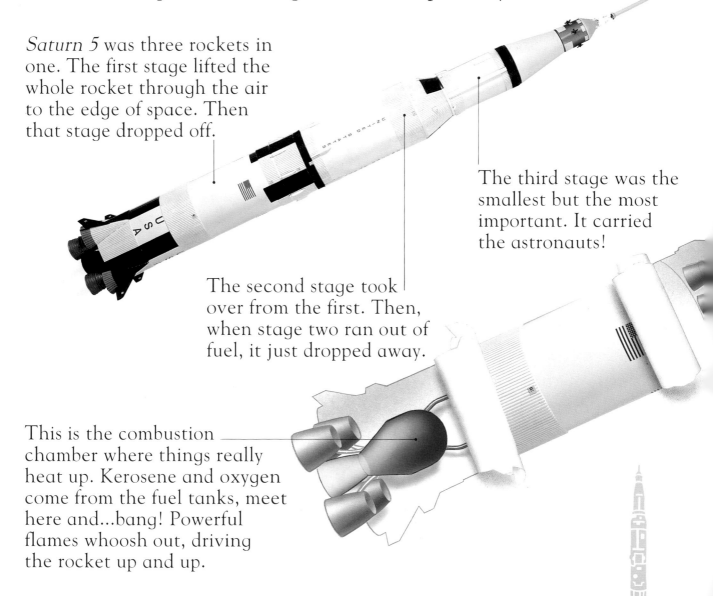

Saturn 5 was three rockets in one. The first stage lifted the whole rocket through the air to the edge of space. Then that stage dropped off.

The third stage was the smallest but the most important. It carried the astronauts!

The second stage took over from the first. Then, when stage two ran out of fuel, it just dropped away.

This is the combustion chamber where things really heat up. Kerosene and oxygen come from the fuel tanks, meet here and...bang! Powerful flames whoosh out, driving the rocket up and up.

COMMAND MODULE

The command module and the lunar module were the only parts of the *Saturn 5* rocket that went all the way to the Moon. The astronauts made their journey to and from the Moon's surface inside the command module.

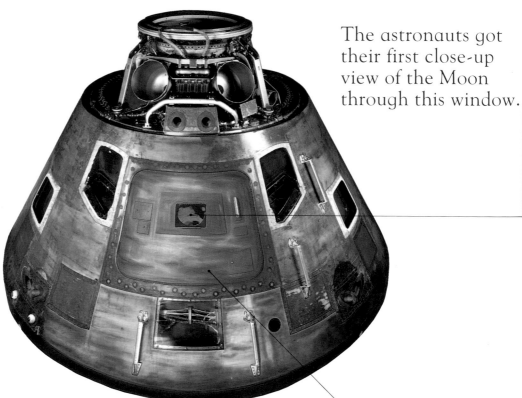

The astronauts got their first close-up view of the Moon through this window.

A thick heat shield protected the command module as it came back through space and hit the blanket of air around the Earth. The module got very hot rubbing against the air as it returned home.

All the astronauts got home safely. They climbed out through this hatch.

Splashdown! These parachutes slowed the module down as it fell toward the sea and a splashy landing!

The lunar module took the astronauts down to the Moon's surface. It was attached here. The crew crawled through this space to get into it from the command module.

These are just two of the motors that were used to steer the module.

The astronauts didn't sit in their seats. They lay down in them so they wouldn't have that funny feeling you sometimes get riding in a roller coaster.

The instrument panel, with lots of complicated knobs and dials, was on the ceiling.

LUNAR MODULE

Neil Armstrong and Buzz Aldrin were the first men on the Moon. They landed there in this lunar landing module on July 20, 1969.

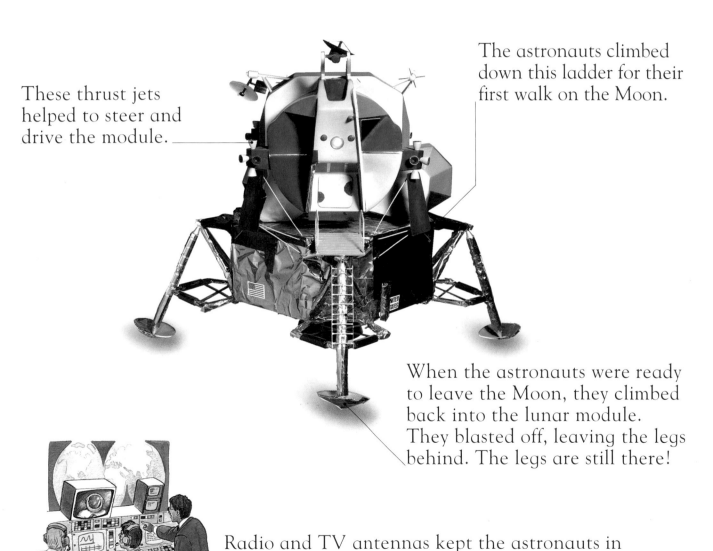

The astronauts climbed down this ladder for their first walk on the Moon.

These thrust jets helped to steer and drive the module.

When the astronauts were ready to leave the Moon, they climbed back into the lunar module. They blasted off, leaving the legs behind. The legs are still there!

Radio and TV antennas kept the astronauts in touch with the command module and with ground control thousands of miles away on Earth.

Using the controls on this panel, the astronauts were able to steer the module – a touch here and a touch there – so they would land in just the right spot.

They've arrived on the Moon's surface. The astronauts put on their space suits before they went out to explore.

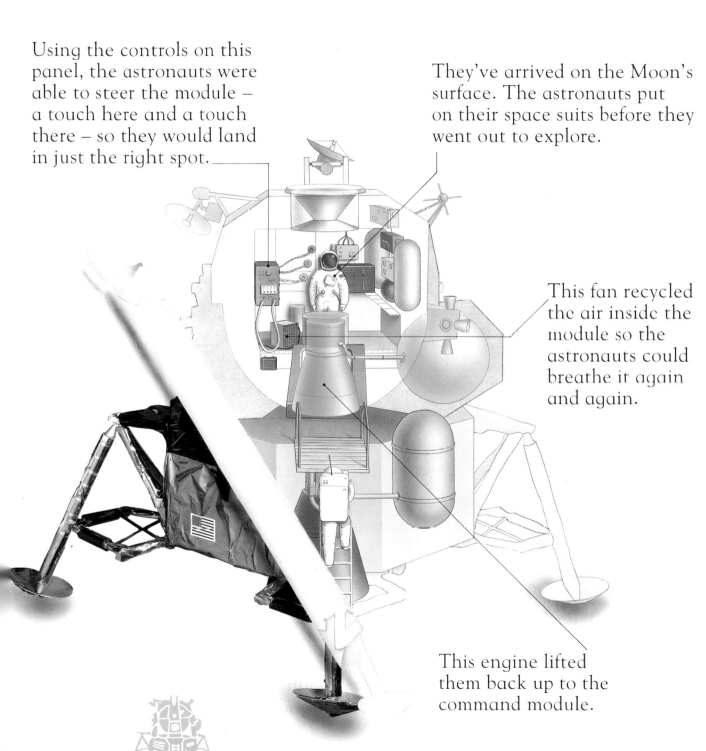

This fan recycled the air inside the module so the astronauts could breathe it again and again.

This engine lifted them back up to the command module.

SPACE SUIT

No one could survive in space without a space suit. Each suit has its own air supply so the astronaut can breathe. It also protects the astronaut from the sun's harmful rays and from bits of rock that fly around in space.

This pack is called a PLSS – a Portable Life Support System. Inside there is oxygen, water, a radio transmitter and a lot of important wires and pipes.

Here is the control panel for the PLSS.

The space suit has enough oxygen and water to keep an astronaut alive for six hours.

The original Moon boots! They are weighted down with heavy metal to make walking on the Moon possible.

So what did the astronauts find when they landed on the Moon? From the rock samples they collected, we know there are valuable minerals up there. Maybe one day there will be mines on the Moon.

Inside the helmet, there is a small microphone and a headset so the astronaut can stay in touch at all times.

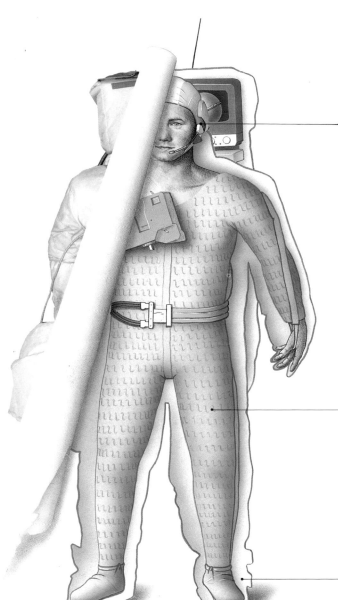

How long does it take you to get dressed in the morning? Neil Armstrong took half an hour to put this suit on – and he needed help.

It's hot work stomping around the Moon in a space suit. The inner layer is a cooling suit with cold water carried all around in little plastic pipes.

The outer layer is padded to give protection against flying rocks.

SPACE SHUTTLE

The shuttle takes off like a rocket and lands back on Earth like a glider. It is boosted up into space with the help of two rockets and a huge fuel tank. While the shuttle is in orbit, it may be used to help launch a new satellite.

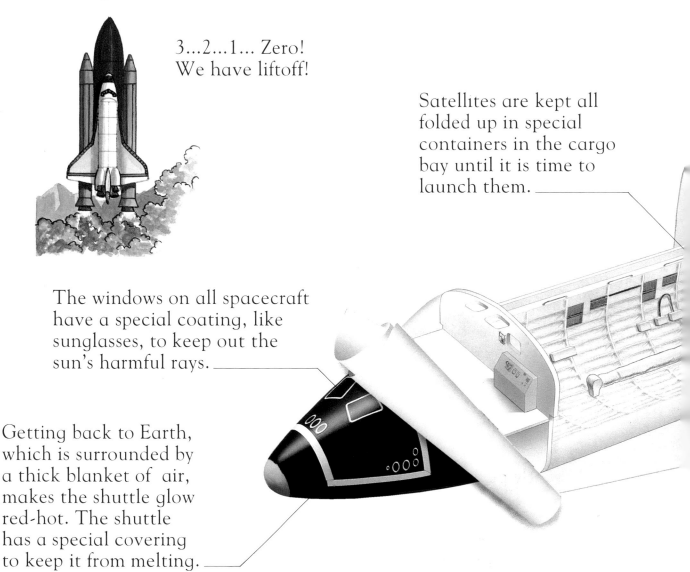

3...2...1... Zero!
We have liftoff!

Satellites are kept all folded up in special containers in the cargo bay until it is time to launch them.

The windows on all spacecraft have a special coating, like sunglasses, to keep out the sun's harmful rays.

Getting back to Earth, which is surrounded by a thick blanket of air, makes the shuttle glow red-hot. The shuttle has a special covering to keep it from melting.

The doors to the cargo bay open out. The shuttle can cruise around in space with them open.

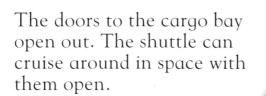

This satellite may be the very one that is beaming down your TV signal or helping you make phone calls to other countries.

These rocket motors steer the shuttle when it is floating in space.

This arm gently pushes the satellites out. When they are floating free, all the antennas, radio dishes, and solar panels unfold.

The shuttle lands on Earth using air currents in the same way a glider does. That's why the shuttle has wings.

The three astronauts are here in their command module. It's tiny compared with the whole rocket.

Because there's no air in space, there's no oxygen, so each stage has to carry its own supply. This is an oxygen tank.

This is a kerosene tank.

Gravity holds everything in place on Earth. Without it, you wouldn't come back to Earth when you jump up in the air.

SHUTTLE CABIN

Up to eight astronauts can live and work in the space shuttle as it travels through space. They can stay there for about a week, carrying out experiments, launching satellites, and taking pictures of stars and planets. Their cabin is in the nose.

Imagine trying to drink a glass of weightless juice! Liquids float around like balls if they are poured from the container, so astronauts drink from the package, using a straw.

Eating ordinary food is out of the question – it won't stay on your plate! Astronauts eat from special packages. The food is made sticky so it stays on the spoon.

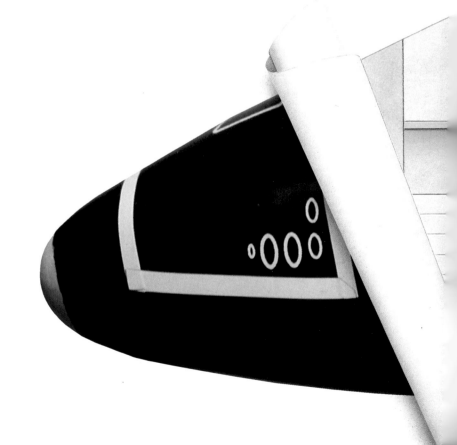

Astronauts wear ordinary clothes inside the shuttle. They don't have to wear helmets because the cabin is filled with normal air.

Astronauts working at the control panel on the flight deck stay in one place by using special footholds on the floor.

There's no point lying down in space because there's no up and no down. At bedtime, just climb inside a sleeping bag and hang yourself on a hook on the wall so you won't float away with your dreams.

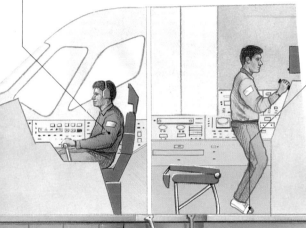

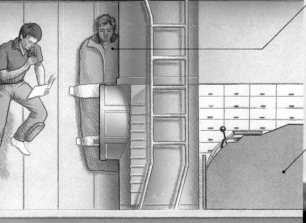

The bathroom has special handgrips and uses air currents instead of water to flush.

SPACELAB

The shuttle can carry a special laboratory and workshop in its cargo bay. It is called Spacelab. On some flights, Spacelab has cages for monkeys and rats so that scientists can study animal behavior in space. Or it can be set up like a medical laboratory for doing work on making new medicines.

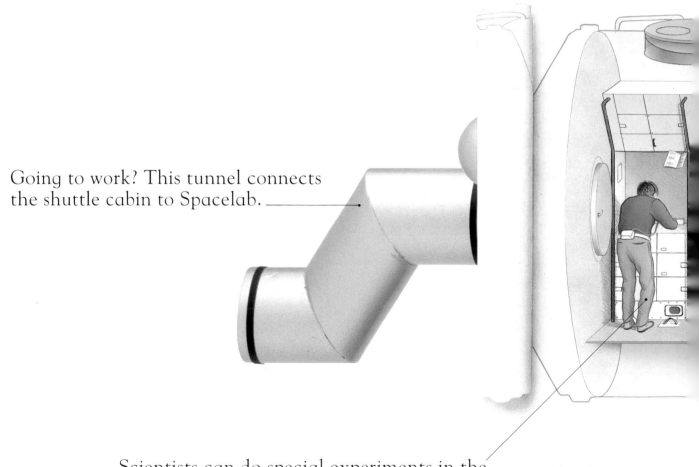

Going to work? This tunnel connects the shuttle cabin to Spacelab.

Scientists can do special experiments in the weightlessness of space. They can make super-strong metals that can't be made on Earth.

Spiders have been taken into space in a laboratory. At first they couldn't figure out how to spin their webs, but they soon learned!

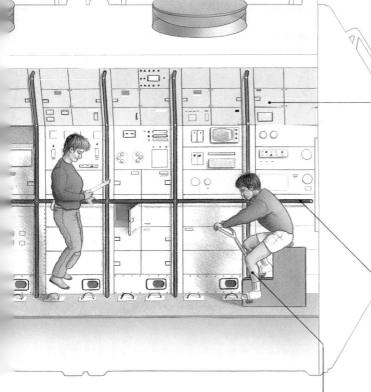

In Spacelab, everything has to be carefully stowed, or it will float away. There are lockers everywhere!

Workbenches have handrails beside them, just in case the scientists start to float away from their work!

Time for some exercise! If you float around weightless for a long time, your bones and muscles get weak because they have no work to do. This exercise machine helps the astronauts to keep fit.

SPACE STATION

This is the Russian space station *Mir*. It is made up of six joined-up laboratories. It stays in space all the time, going round and round Earth. The astronauts come and go in special spacecraft.

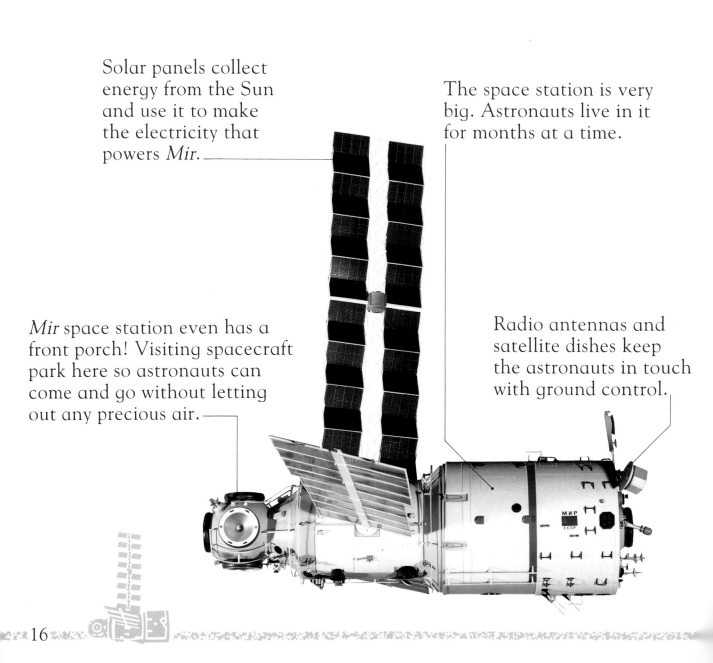

Solar panels collect energy from the Sun and use it to make the electricity that powers *Mir*.

The space station is very big. Astronauts live in it for months at a time.

Mir space station even has a front porch! Visiting spacecraft park here so astronauts can come and go without letting out any precious air.

Radio antennas and satellite dishes keep the astronauts in touch with ground control.

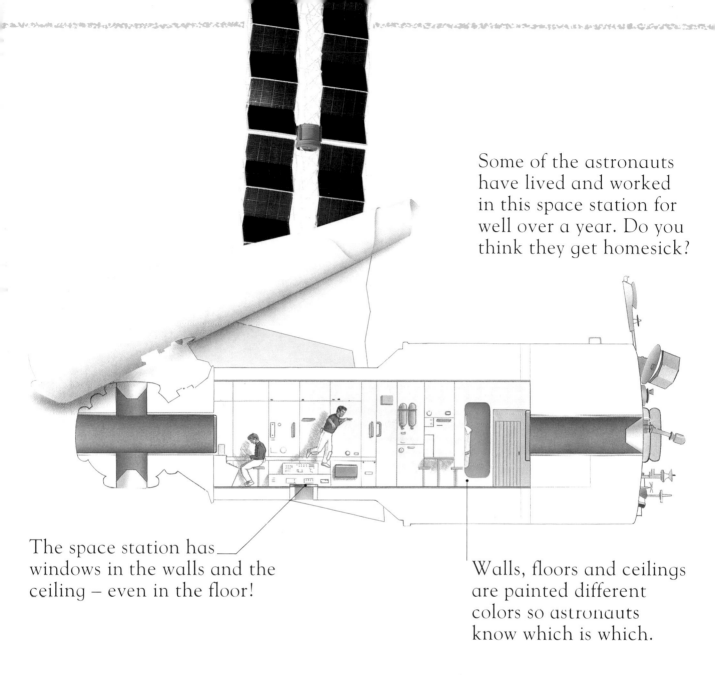

Some of the astronauts have lived and worked in this space station for well over a year. Do you think they get homesick?

The space station has windows in the walls and the ceiling – even in the floor!

Walls, floors and ceilings are painted different colors so astronauts know which is which.

From time to time, ground control sends up a spacecraft loaded with food, spare parts, and letters from home. These parcel-post spacecraft fly all by themselves, with no one at the controls!

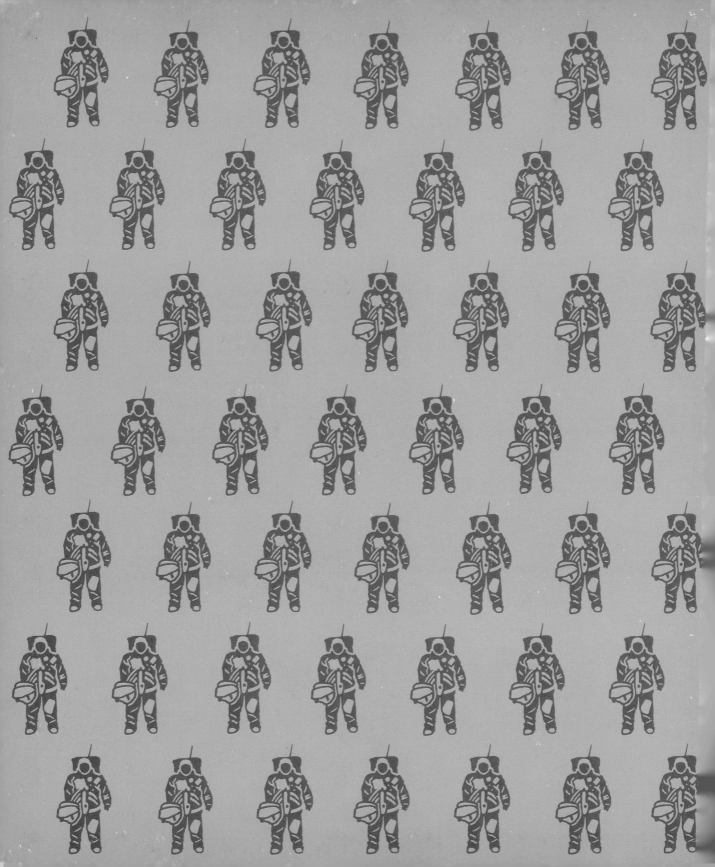